MESQUITE DUNES

A SINUOUS SYMPHONY WRITTEN ON A ANCIENT DRY LAKE

IMAGES BY JOHN AYDELOTTE

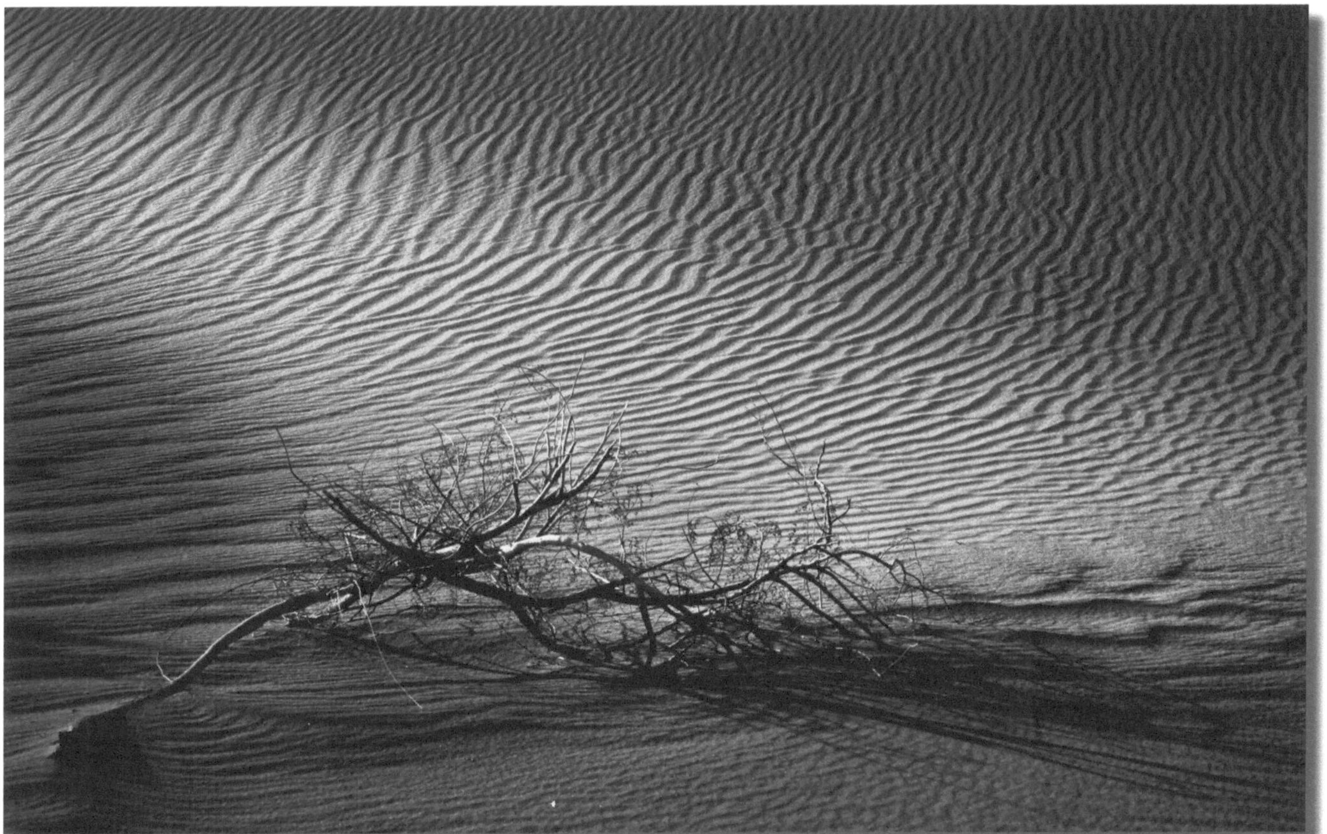

ISBN-13: 978-1512357066
ISBN-10: 1512357065

MESQUITE DUNES

A SINUOUS SYMPHONY WRITTEN ON A ANCIENT DRY LAKE

Images Words and Processing by John Aydelotte

Special thanks to my Friend, Mentor and Teacher from the Arcanum Rodney Campbell for his help and advice throughout this project. Without his input and encouragement this project may of never been completed. The image contained on the following pages were recorded in the past few years using digital imaging.

About the Author

John Aydelotte is a tireless photographer with years of photographic background. Starting a career in photography almost 40 years ago John has made his living from photography. John freelanced for a couple of years then opened a commercial studio and built a clientele of several large corporations, graphic artists, local businesses and advertising agencies. John operated the studio successfully for years only closing due to a injury that made working at a fast pace impossible. John continued to work in photography and Graphics at a then small company which he helped to grow to a mid size company for the next 15 years at which time in 2014 he retired. Upon retirement he has retrained and started to image what he feels in his heart to be his fullest creative endeavor. John was always a outdoors person and now he has the time to image and share the images that come from within his heart.

The Sand Dunes are mystical to me. Over 40 years ago I made a photography trip to Death Valley. At that time I carried a 4x5 camera into the dunes exposing several sheets of film. What those sheets of film contained kindled a my love for photography. I developed and printed those images and they have hung on my wall for years. I had read about the masters of photography and their experiences in the dunes and I could then and still do feel their presence when I am in the dunes. I had not shot in the dunes for over 35 five years after that trip only returning in 2013. The magic is still there but now days a lot of people are present so I pick my times when I shoot very carefully. I don't only shoot dunes and image almost anywhere at any time of day and even night. For those beginning there journey in photography I have included camera lens and exposure data for each image. I caution you that it is not the camera or the lens it is much more the vision of the photographer. For me I look first for the light then I work on subject and composition if it is not right I may move on or if I feel there is something there I will make several images until I know I have what is the best possible image. Photography is about feeling and the excitement of a great image. I used to be mechanical in my commercial studio as things had to match but shooting landscape I can put my feelings into each and every shot. I feel it is true that the camera sees two directions.

For my process I image in color and use the color information to make my black and white images using Lightroom and Photoshop. Many times I know an image will be black and white before exposure. It has taken me years to visualize in black and white with color being so present at the time of exposure. I also shoot color only images but almost always with a plan or visualization of some sort. Black and white images involve the viewer so they invoke thoughts. Black and white is like a fine book as opposed to a movie. The movie shows you everything but the book lets you supply the visuals. When you look at the image in this book let your mind wonder and feel the mood and textures. Imagine walking in the blowing sand with the sand hitting your legs. Think about a walk at night in the dunes or a climb to the top of a tall dune. Think about the constant change of the dunes. Most of all enjoy what you see.

John Aydelotte

Camera Data

Page 1 Branching Out
Camera: Sony A7r
Lens: Sony FE 70-200mm F4 G at 104mm
Exposure: 1/80 sec. at f16 ISO 100

Page 7 Dune Detail with Shadow
Camera: Sony A7r
Lens: Sony FE 70-200mm F4 G at 70mm
Exposure: 1/30 sec. at f16 ISO 100

Page 8 Alone at the Top
Camera: Sony A7r
Lens: Sony FE 70-200mm F4 G at 200mm
Exposure: 1/125 sec. at f16 ISO 400

Page 9 Bushes on Dune
Camera: Sony A7r
Lens: Sony FE 70-200mm F4 G at 85mm
Exposure: 1/100 sec. at f16 ISO 100

Page 10 Blowing Sand and Ripples
Camera: Sony A99
Lens: Sony 24-70mm F2.8 ZA at 45mm
Exposure: 1/60 sec. at f8 ISO 100

Page 11 Lone Bush in Sand Storm
Camera: Sony A99
Lens: Sony 24-70mm F2.8 ZA at 70mm
Exposure: 1/50 sec. at f16 ISO 1000

Page 12-13 top Dune Sunrise Panorama
Camera: Sony A7r
Lens: Sony FE 70-200mm F4 G at 110mm
Exposure: 1/50 sec. at f8 ISO 100

Page 12-13 bottom Dune Curve Panorama
Camera: Sony A7r
Lens: Sony FE 70-200mm F4 G at 200mm
Exposure: 1/13 sec. at f11 ISO 100

Page 14 Branches in Sand
Camera: Sony A99
Lens: Sony 24-70mm F2.8 ZA at 60mm
Exposure: 3.2 sec. at f8 ISO 100

Page 15 Dune Tracks
Camera: Sony A7r
Lens: Sony FE 70-200mm F4 G at 116mm
Exposure: 1/100 sec. at f16 ISO 100

Page 16 Dunescape Evening Light
Camera: Sony A7r
Lens: Sony FE 70-200mm F4 G at 85mm
Exposure: 1/100 sec. at f16 ISO 100

Page 17 Dunescape 4
Camera: Sony A7r
Lens: Sony FE 24-70mm F4 ZA at 57mm
Exposure: 1/30 sec. at f16 ISO 100

Page 18 Pre Sunrise
Camera: Sony A7r
Lens: Sony FE 70-200mm F4 G at 200mm
Exposure: .6 sec. at f4 ISO 800

Page 19 Snaky Dune at First Sun
Camera: Sony A99
Lens: Sony 24-70mm F2.8 ZA at 60mm
Exposure: 1/60 sec. at f8 ISO 100

Page 20 Dunes and Funeral Mts.
Camera: Sony A99
Lens: Sony 24-70mm F2.8 ZA at 55mm
Exposure: 1/200 sec. at f10 ISO 100

Page 21 Afternoon Dunescape
Camera: Sony A7r
Lens: Sony FE 70-200mm F4 G at 70mm
Exposure: 1/160 sec. at f16 ISO 400

Page 22 100 Degrees
Camera: Sony A7r
Lens: Sony FE 24-70mm F4 ZA at 70mm
Exposure: 1/8 sec. at f22 ISO 80

Page 23 Sunset Quite Light
Camera: Sony A7r
Lens: Sony FE 70-200mm F4 G at 70mm
Exposure: 1/100 sec. at f16 ISO 400

Page 24 Night in the Dunes
Camera: Sony A7r
Lens: Sony FE 16-35mm F4 ZA at 16mm
Exposure Stars: 25 sec. at f4 ISO 16000
Exposure Foreground*: 25 sec. at f4 ISO 100
* Foreground lighting done with flashlight

THE MESQUITE DUNES

I am drawn to their aesthetic purity.
I see their graceful curves and forms.
I see the highlights and shadows at both ends of the day.
I see the life and activity in the small surface markings.
I see the slow change from day to day and year to year.
I see the sand hopping across the surface when the wind blows.
I see the flat that they are built on by the wind and sands of death valley.
I see the mounds and ridges move like waves in the wind.
I see the large ripples of course grains of sand and the small textures of the fine grain.
I see the peaks, the valleys and the lobes of flowing sand.
Most of all I see the endless cycle of time.
I come with respect and I image with respect.

John Aydelotte

Cover Image: Branch in sand
This image shows the randomness of the ripples and textures to be found in the mesquite dunes. The textures change with the direction of the wind sometimes constantly during robust winds. The larger dunes have a smaller daily change but large changes take years to occur.

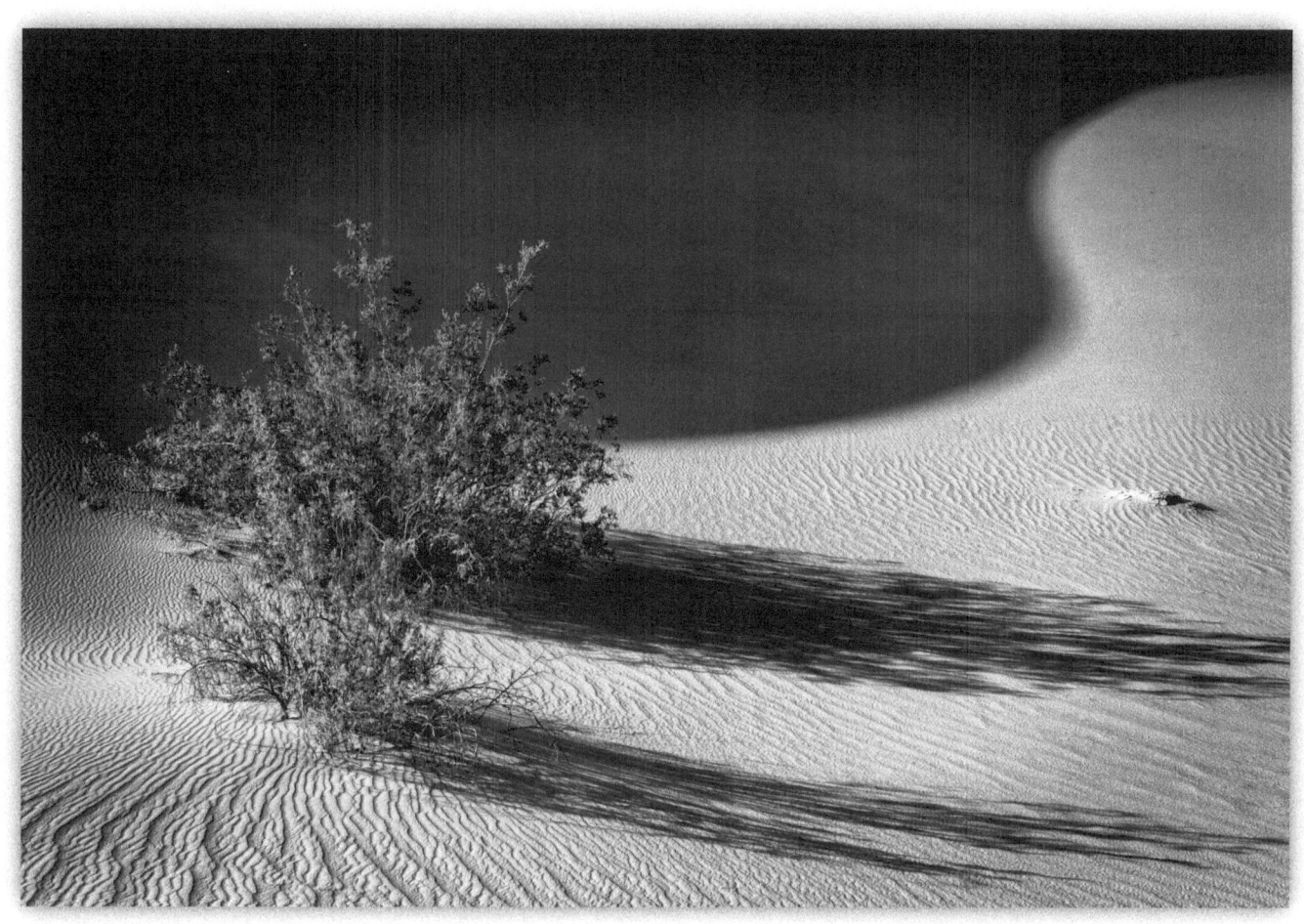

Aesthetic Purity

I shoot from my heart so things like graceful curves existing with textures and the tones of the ever moving sun draw my attention. These creosote bushes with their glimmering seed pods against the a textured sun swept sand and a dark background with the textures disappearing into the shadow of the late afternoon sun was a must to be imaged.

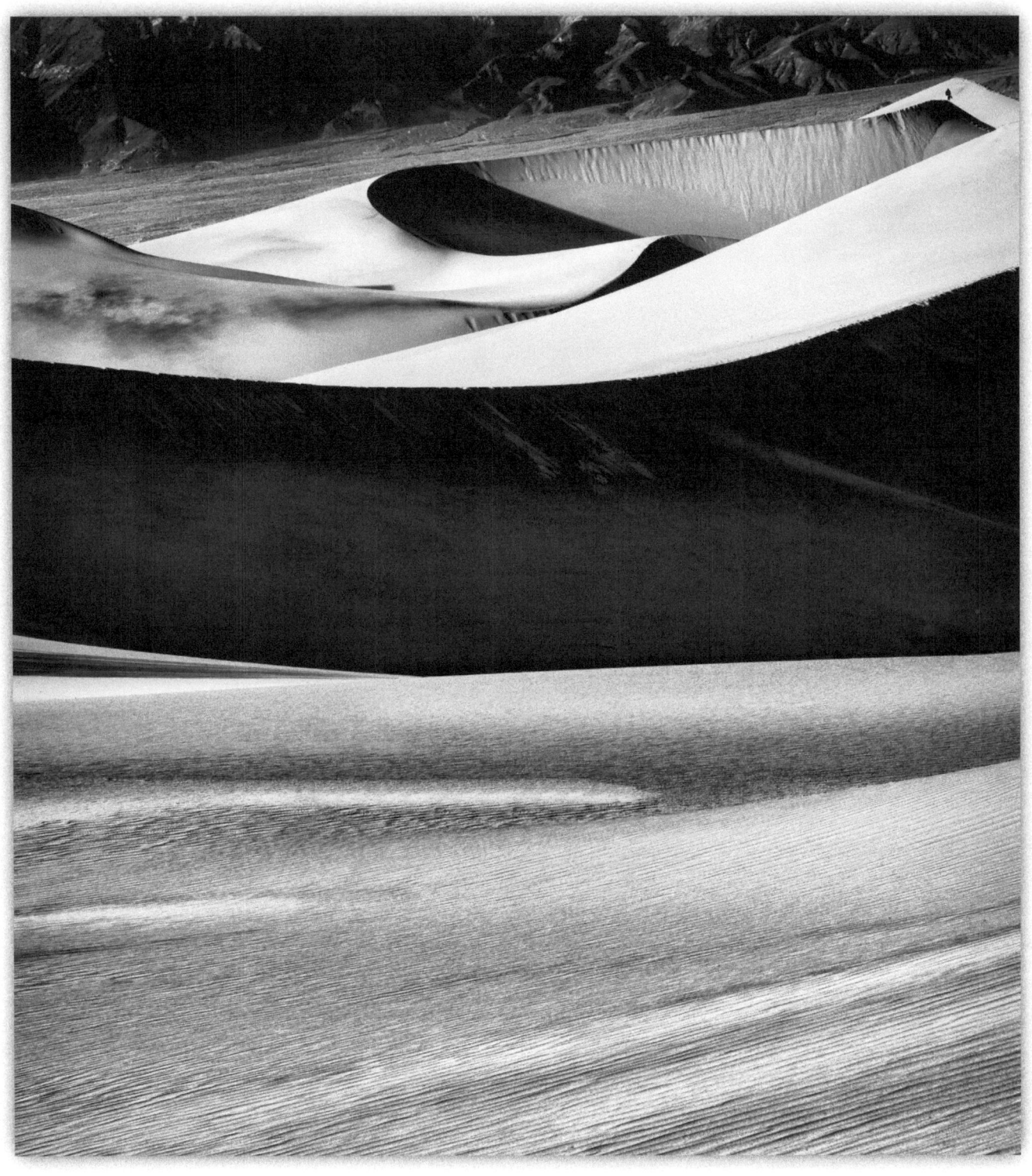

Graceful curves covered with textures and tones from the evening sun. A single individual close to the top gives a sense of scale to the 140 foot high dunes. The distant dunes look to have no texture but that is far from true. The light in the morning only lasts a few minutes before the textures become flat to the eye. In the evening the process is much slower with good light lasting as much as a hour at sometimes of the year. In the center of the dunes the wind blows from 4 directions so the dunes swirl causing center dune to form a star like shape.

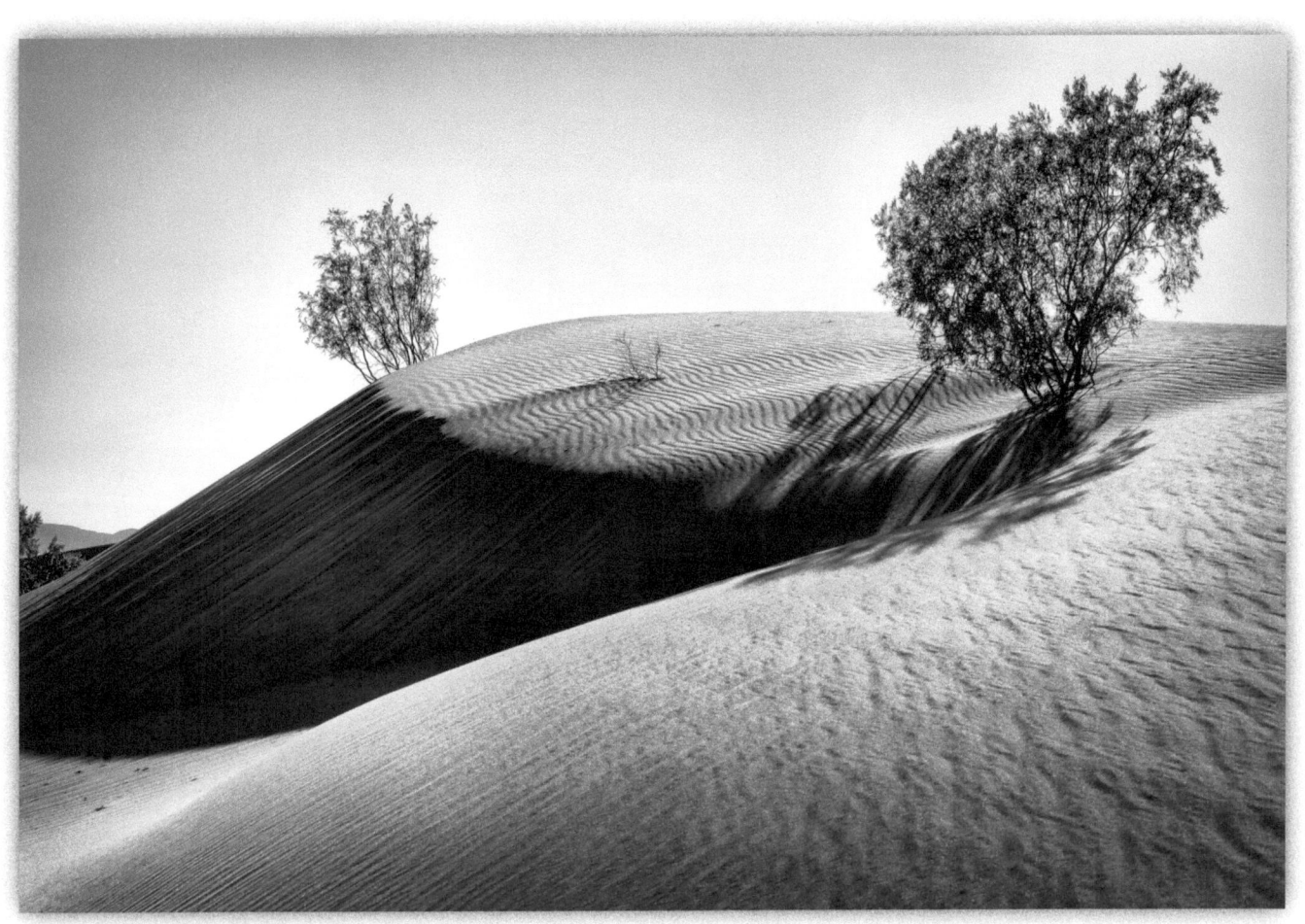

The mesquite dunes have no particular shape but for the most part run in ridges with tucks and folds forming curves and sweeps. This late afternoon image shows the creosote bushes which get their moisture from the water held by the dunes. With an average rainfall of 2 inches life must be tough for the creosote but they seem to do better then the mesquite which send roots down as much as 100 feet into the flat to gather moisture.

CURVES AND FORMS

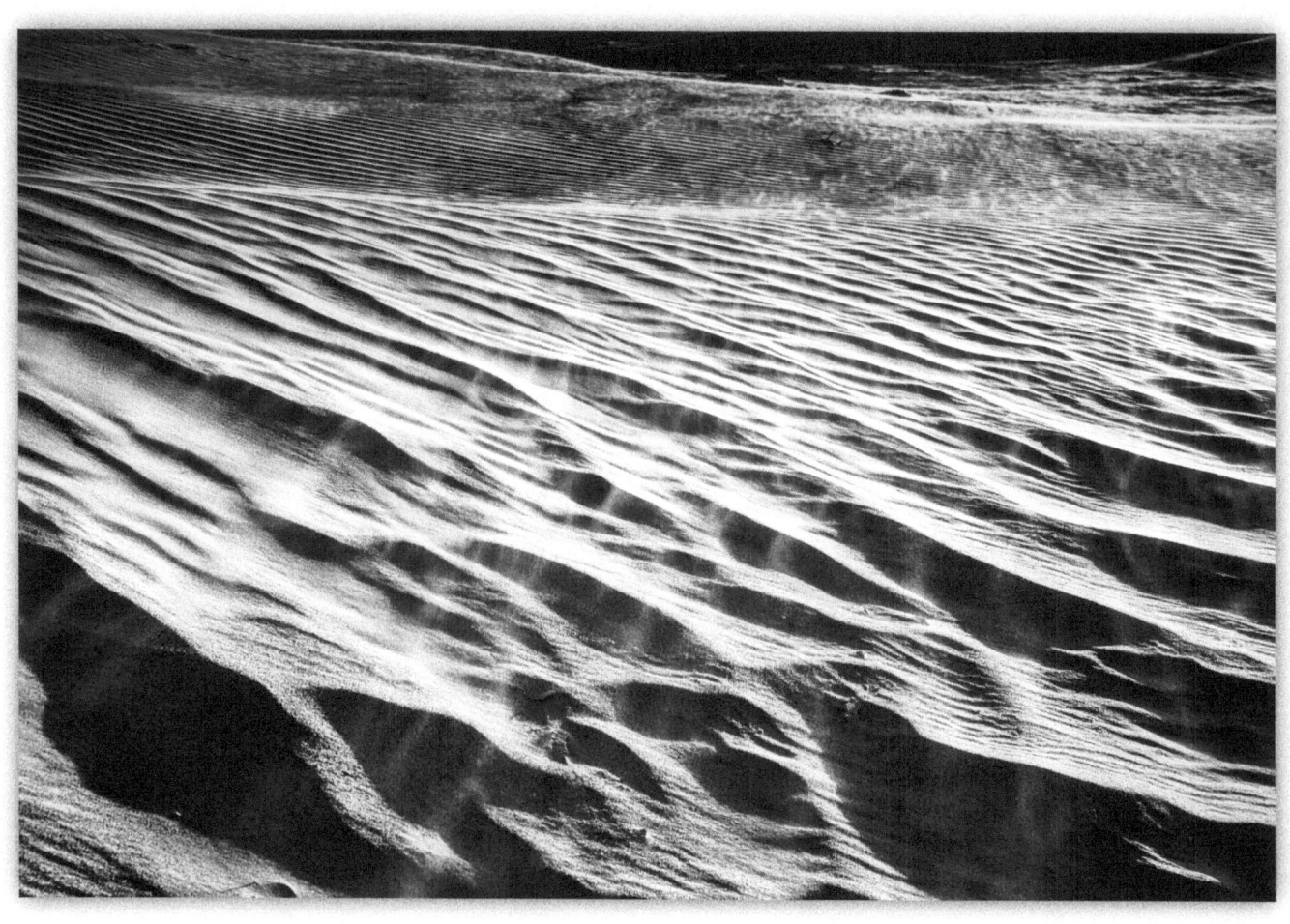

Blowing Sand

This day the winds were very strong. Visibility was not bad as the sand barely rose more then 12 inches above the surface. This image was taken near the resort of Stovepipe Wells. Originally the resort was to be built near the stovepipe well on the other side of the dunes. Things didn't work out as the hard rubber tires on the trucks sunk into the sand so the location was moved to the present day location at Burnt Wagon Point, the area where the Jayhawkers burnt their wagons in 1850 and continued on via foot in their trek to the Gold country in the Sierra foothills.

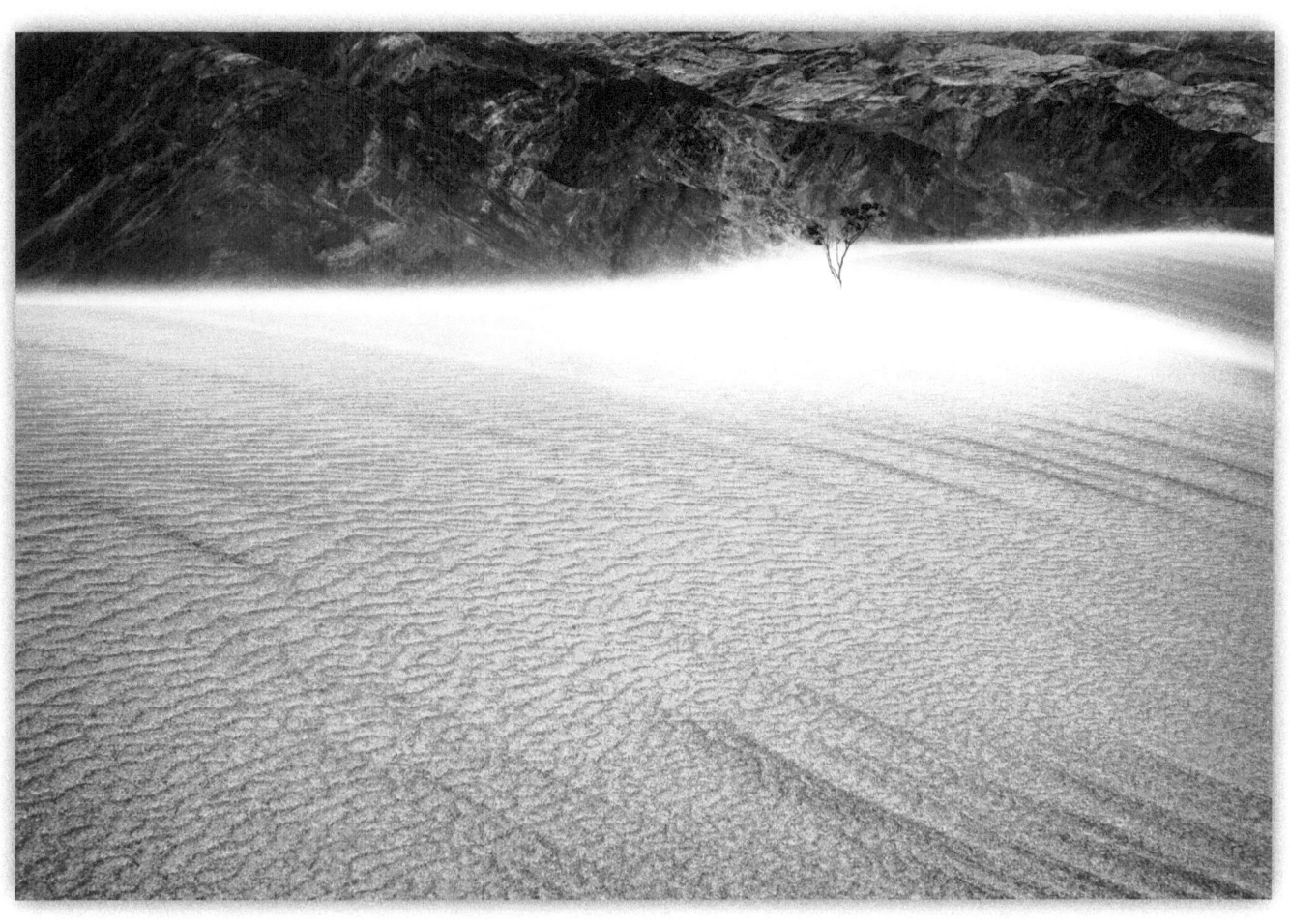

A strong wind blew and the sand moved. The tiny grains of sand hopped along the surface dislodging others along their way. When the sand blows it stays close to the surface never going above about 18 inches. You can feel it on your legs as it preforms a renewal process of erasing footprints and forming new textures.

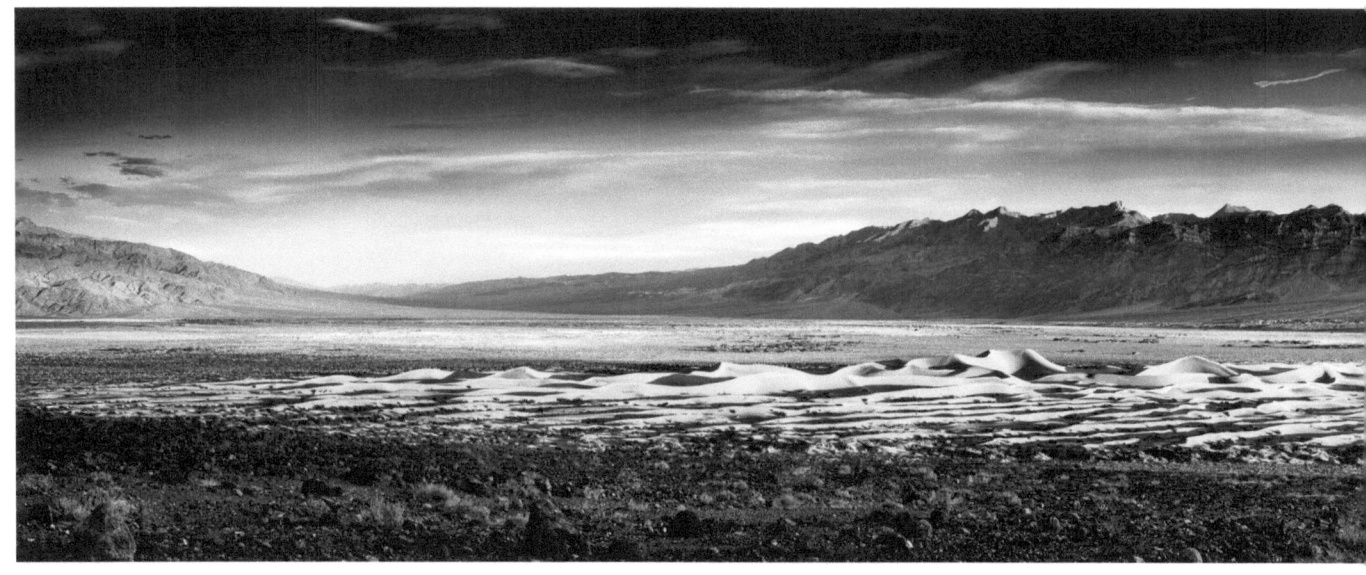

Top: Dune Panorama

This image not only shows the vastness of the mesquité dune system but its relationship to the whole of the northern Death Valley. The dunes are surrounded by mountains and set in a low spot in the center of the valley. The wind blows from all directions and contributes to the dunes from all directions. In the center of the dunes lies the largest dune about 140 feet in height. It is star shaped due to the influence of the multi directional winds.

Waves in the Wind

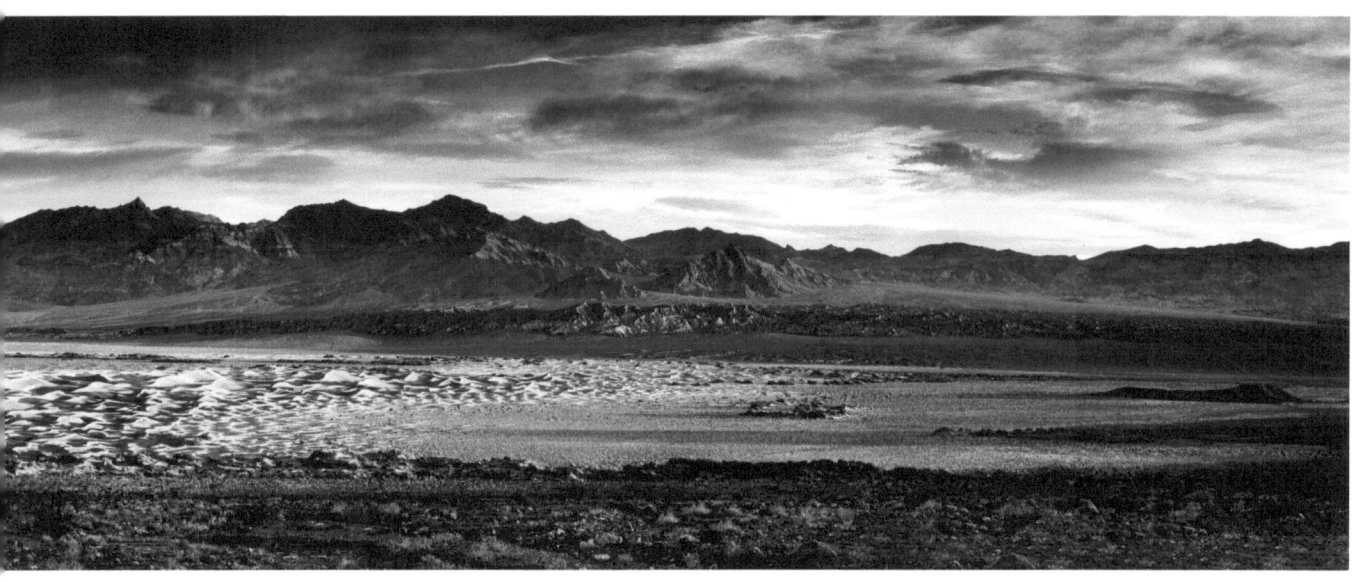

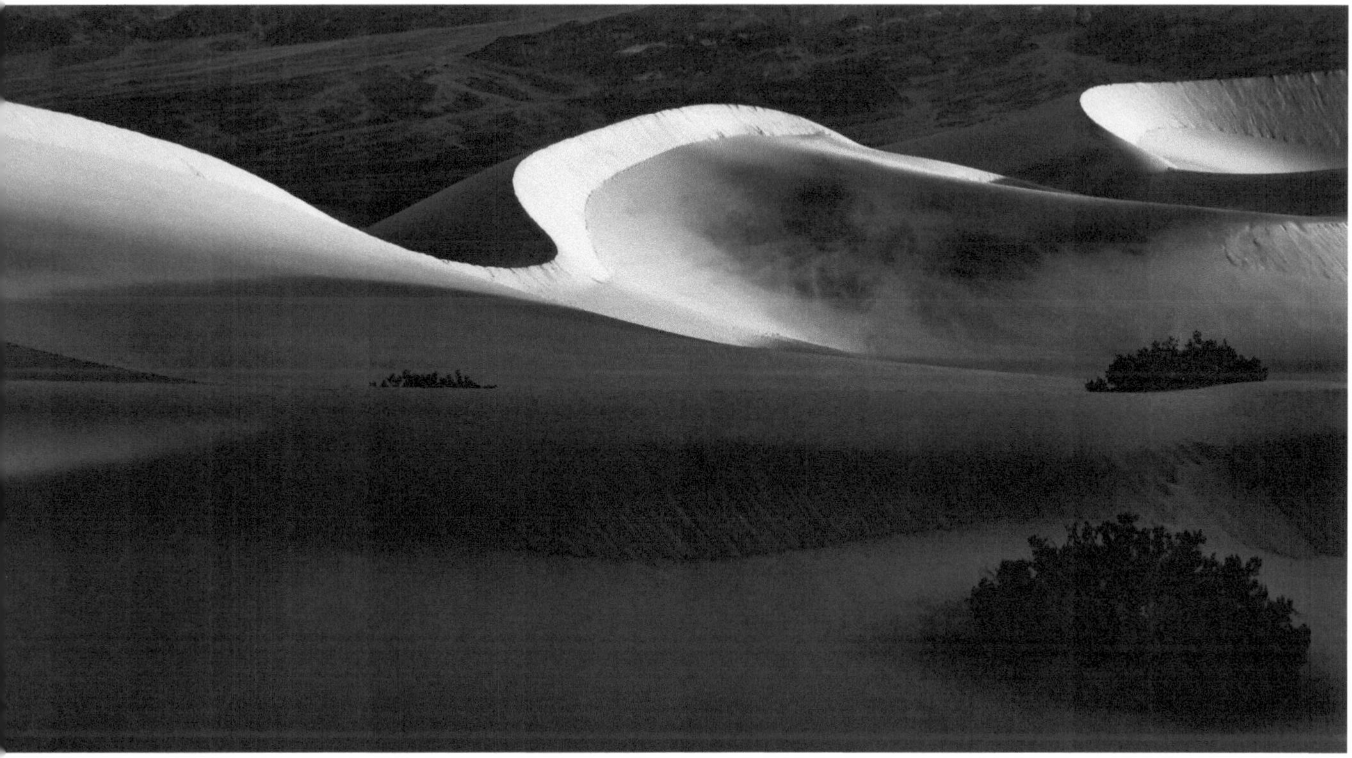

Right: Sinuous Dunes
This ridge runs to the east of the larger center star dune. Most the dunes make
big long ridges and have such wonderful shape and form that they are a much for
photographers. Most the time they are covered with footprints but every so often
a large wind makes an opportunity for photography on a grand scale.

LIFE AND DEATH

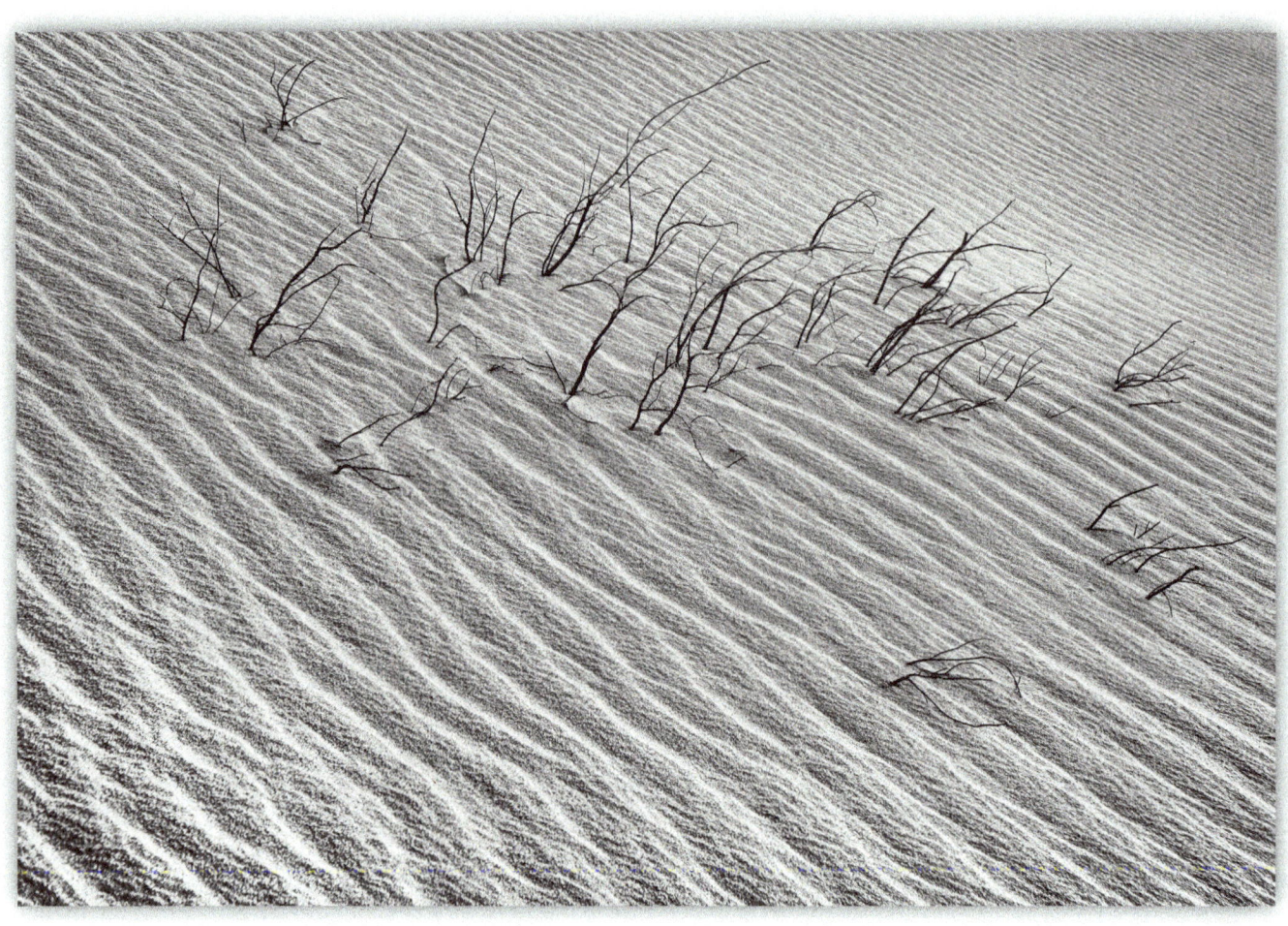

The dunes are alive with vegetation but also they are on the move with every wind. When creosote is covered by the sands or loses it's supply of sun so it dies. As the sand moves the death of a creosote bush may be revealed. There is an abundance of life in the dunes both animal and plant. It is amazing how so much survives in such a changing harsh environment.

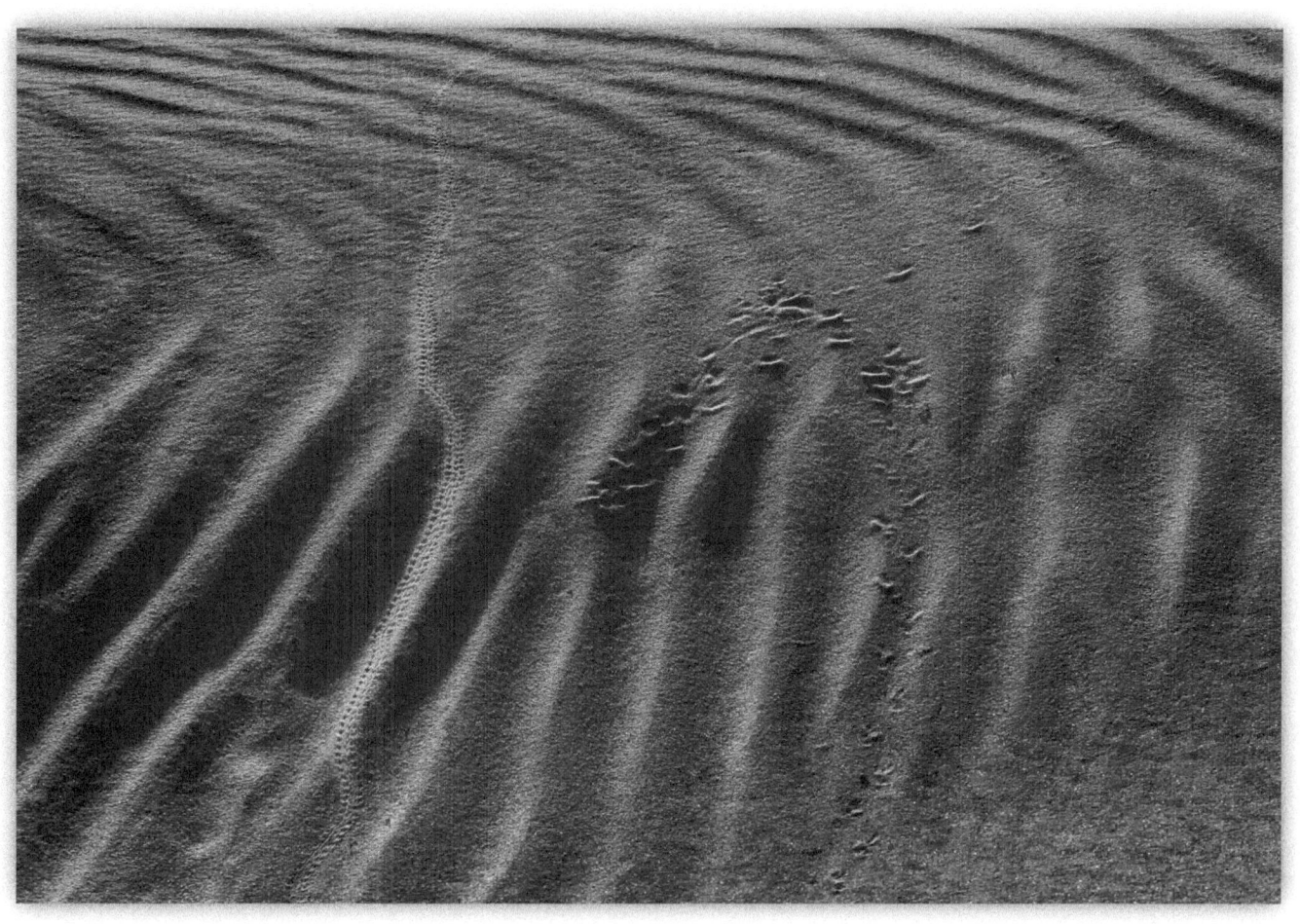

This Image tells a story of life and survival. A kangaroo rat, very common in the dunes, was walking up the dune when all of a sudden he realized that a snake was close. He was panicked then run off to safety. This story occurs everyday in the dunes sometimes the end is different and the snake is the winner. As a photographer it is a joy to record such a scenario that is why I look where I walk in the dunes being careful not to erase such a story.

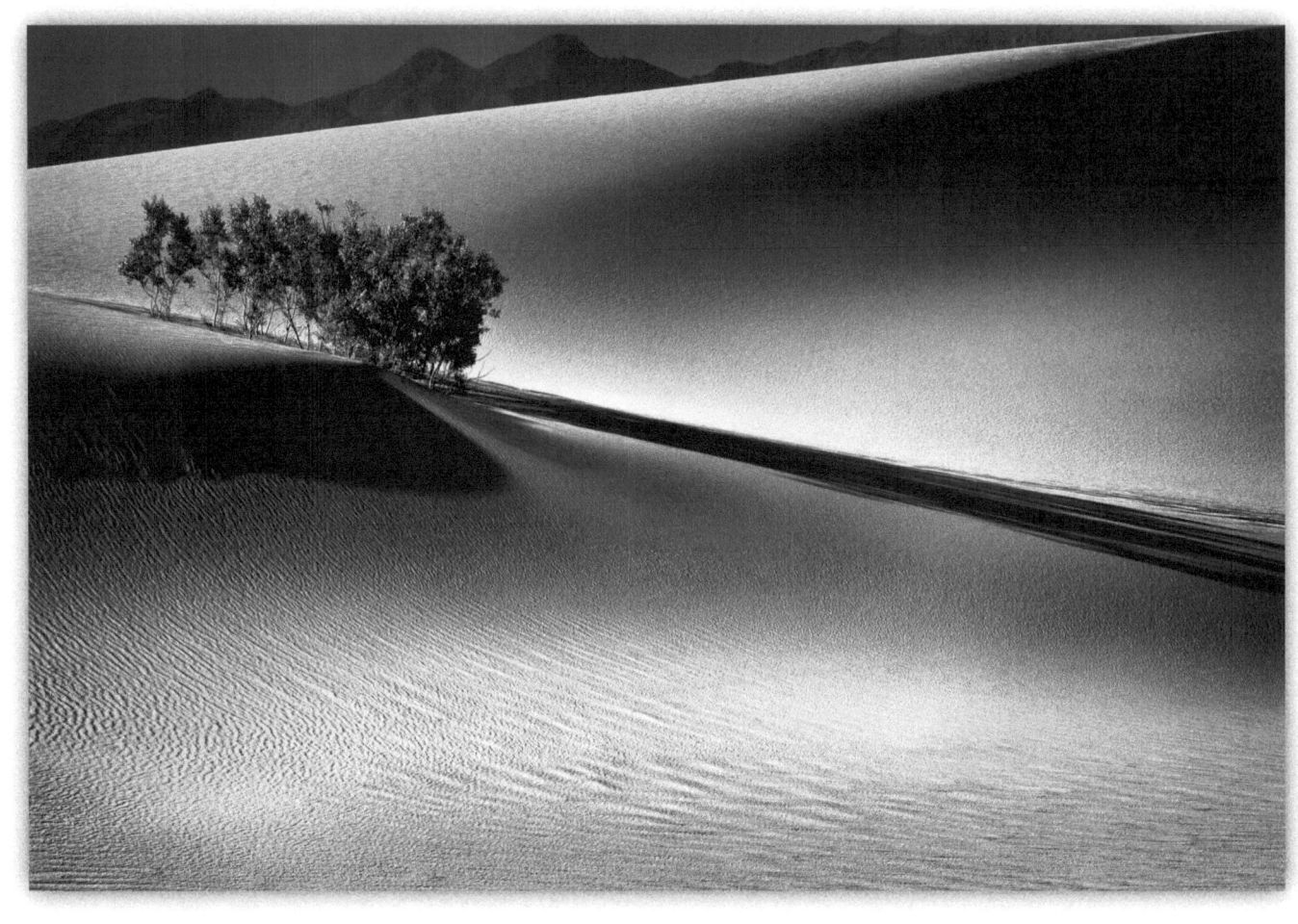

HIGHLIGHT AND SHADOW

The changing light is what photography is about in the dunes. The interaction between the form and shape with the angle of the sun forcing the appearance of textures can make an image suddenly appear and just a quickly disappear. Most of the day there are shadows here and there but very little texture due to the high angle of the sun.

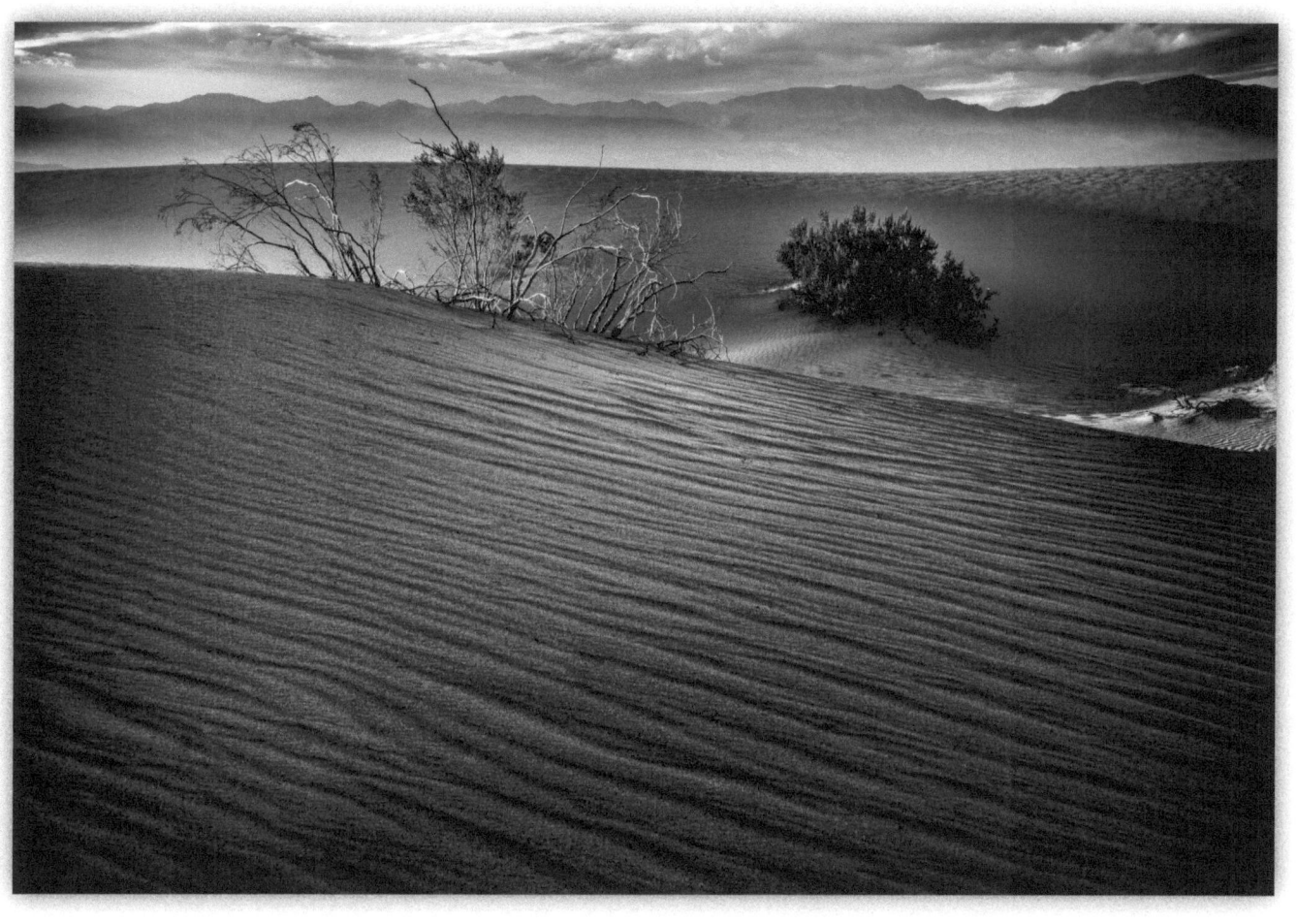

In the mornings and in the evening the dunes take on a whole knew feeling.. Large shapes are still smooth and flowing but now they are covered with texture. With the light skating across the tops of the dunes the feeling of light and shadow is awe inspiring. Every trip I make to Death Valley I try to spend at least one morning or evening in the dunes.

Morning Light

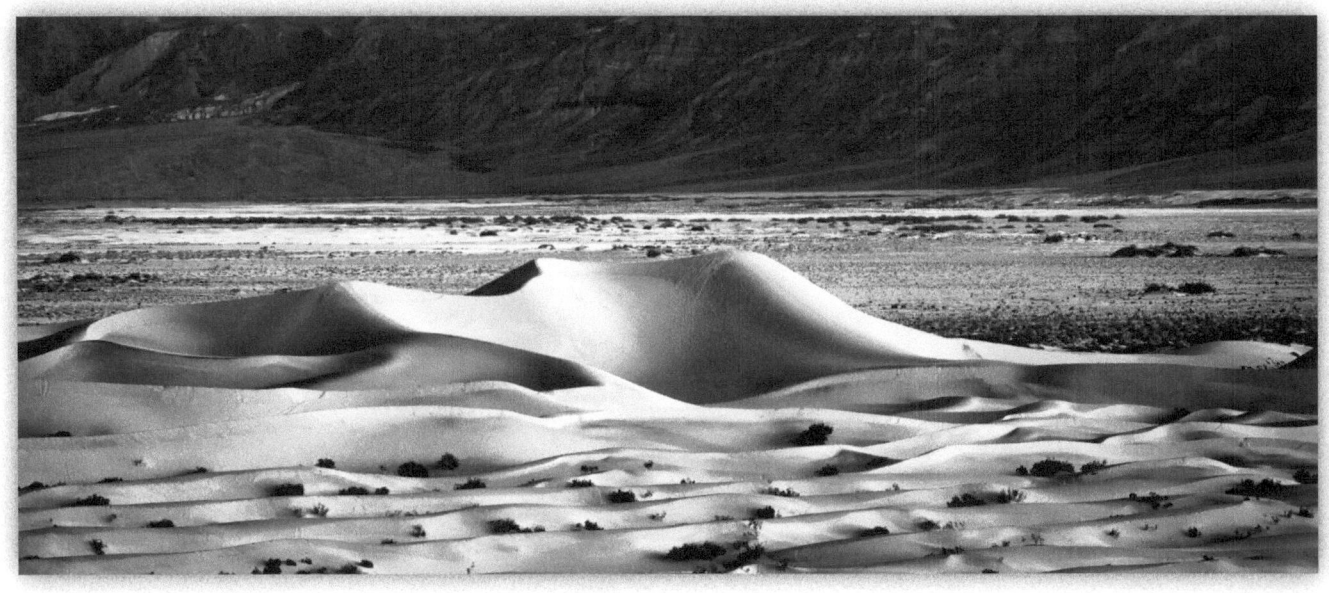

The good morning light in the dunes last only a few minutes, sometimes as short a three minutes if it even happens. The morning sunrise can be spectacular for both close and long distance shooting. This long distance image was captured from high on the hill by the mesquite dunes. When shooting in the dunes you walk in the dark and as the light of day starts to break you setup for a capture and then look around and try to find 1 or 2 more close by then wait for the sun. The morning sun is low and bright and when it breaks you work fast hoping to make 2 or 3 views. The morning sun usually has more color then the evening light so for color work it is very important but also it helps to separate sky lit areas from sun lit in black and white.

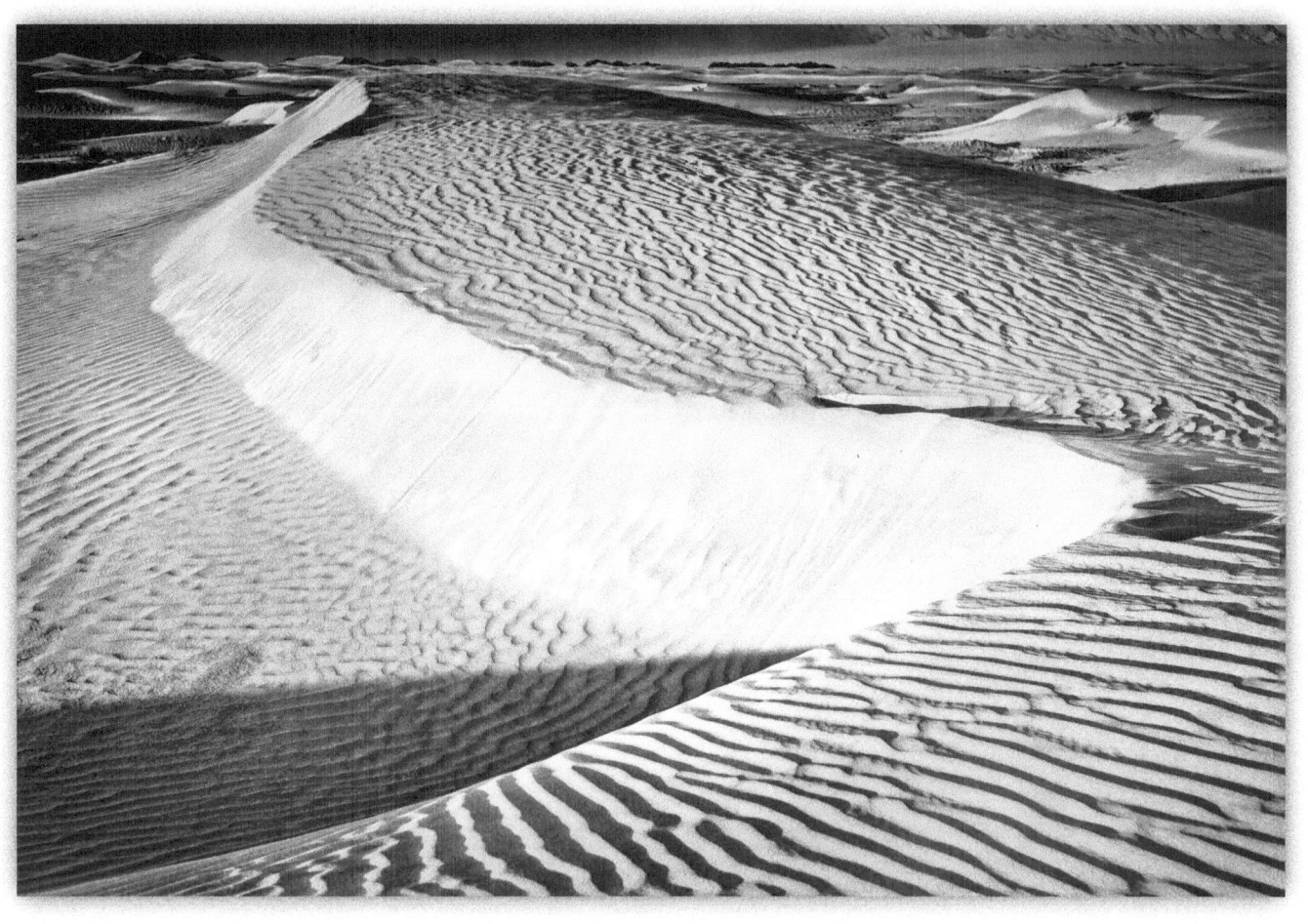

I still remember taking this morning image. The large dunes were full of human tracks so I headed to the short dunes by the old Stovepipe well. I set up for this shot. It was very pink due to the feldspar which is pink in color and then all of a sudden all changes the bright golden sun was just starting to peek over the horizon. I was shocked at the beauty of the color and the texture that was all but lost a minute earlier.

Evening Light

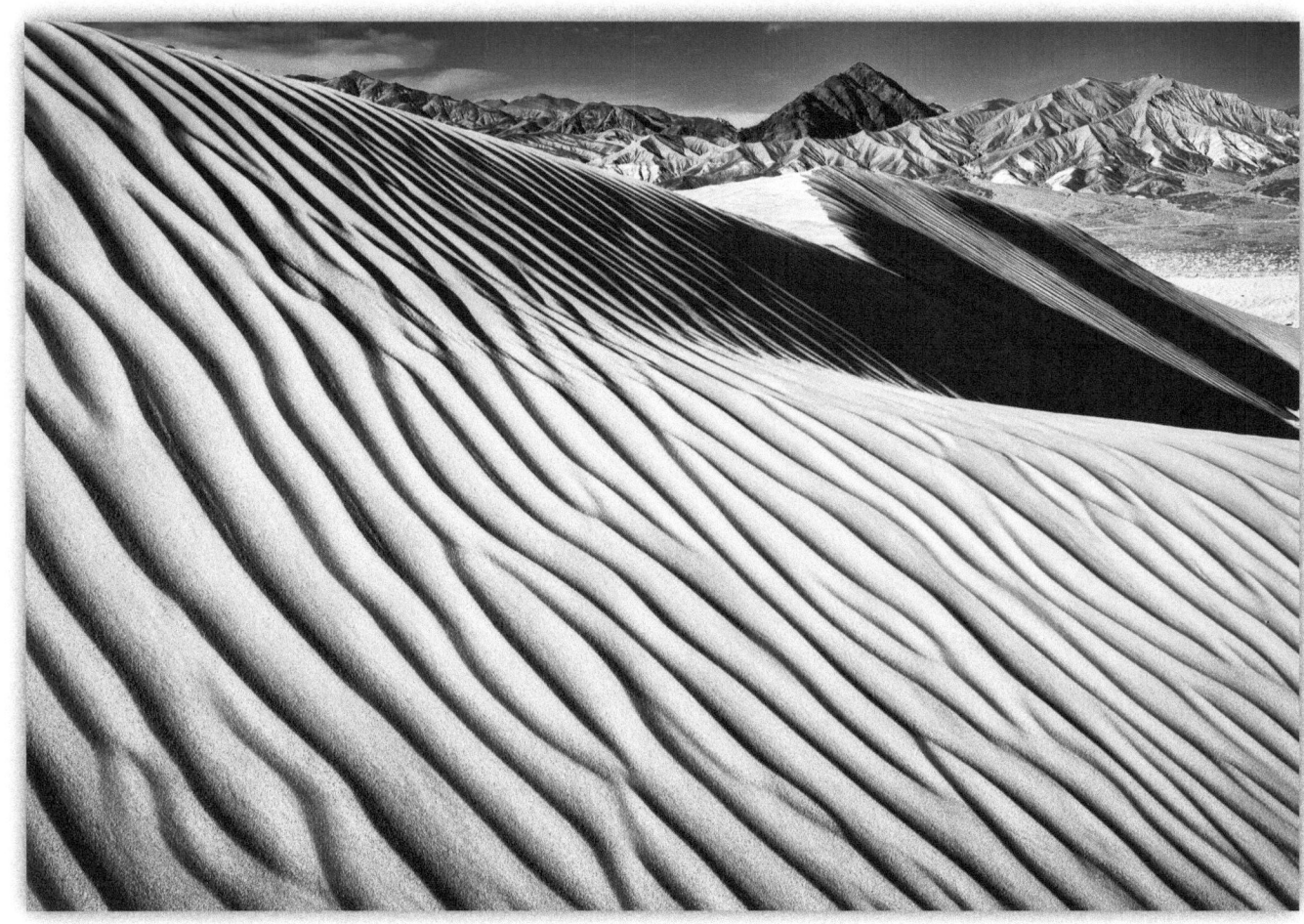

In the late afternoon the sun goes down over a rather high Panamint mountain range. I really don't know why but the light is more gradual at the end of the day then at the beginning. This image was made in the short dunes near stovepipe well and shows the grapevine mountains. In this section the dunes run in long ridges with wide flat areas between the ridges. This image was taken close to the end of one such ridge.

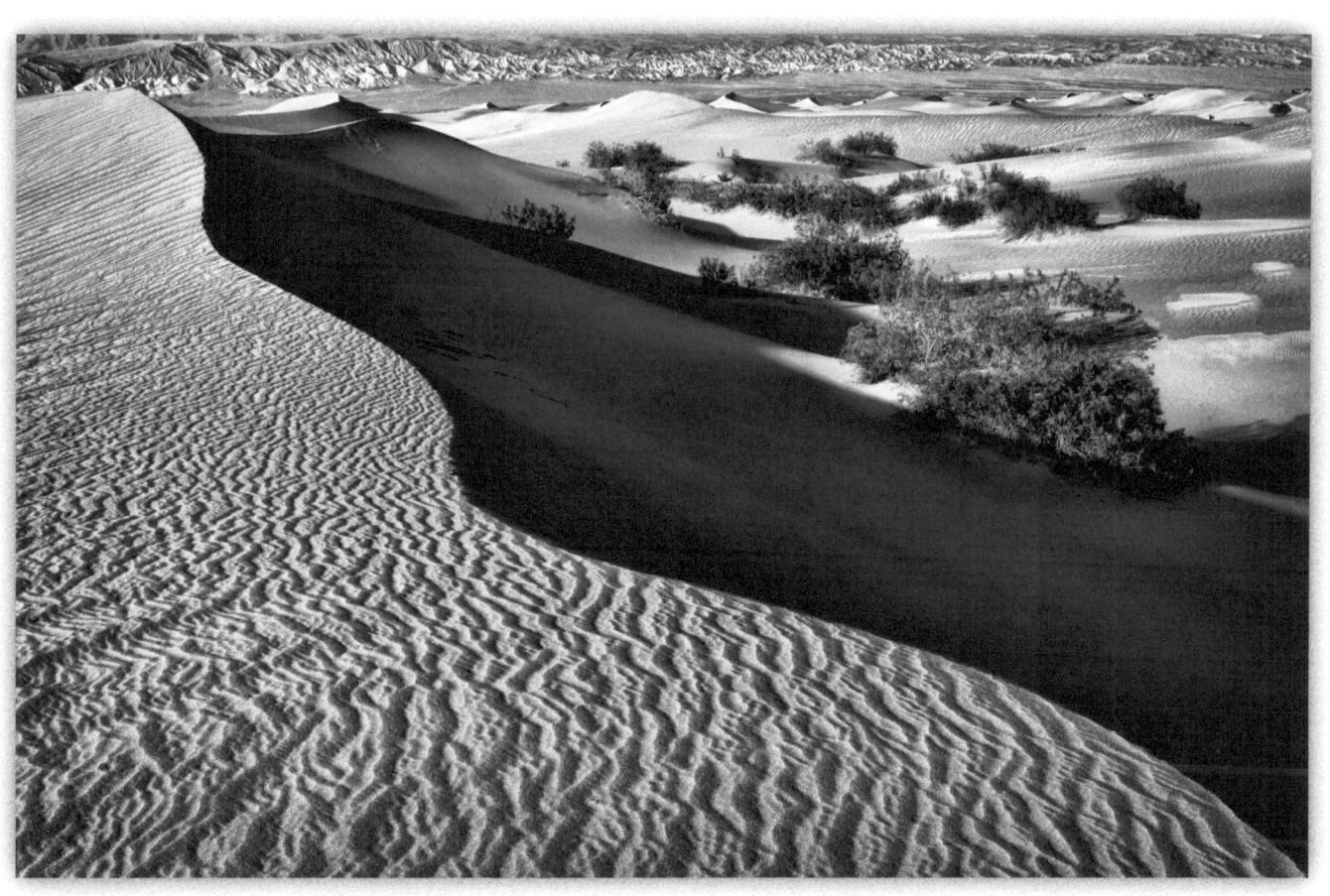

A very strong wind had blown the day before and wiped the dunes clean of footprints. The ridges were smooth and only a few feet had been in the dunes that day. Textures both large and small were revealed and the larger feldspar crystals were showing. Everything was so crisp including the air. You wish times like this would last longer but they won't, in fact the next few days were very hazy and enough so that this shot could not be duplicated.

END OF DAY

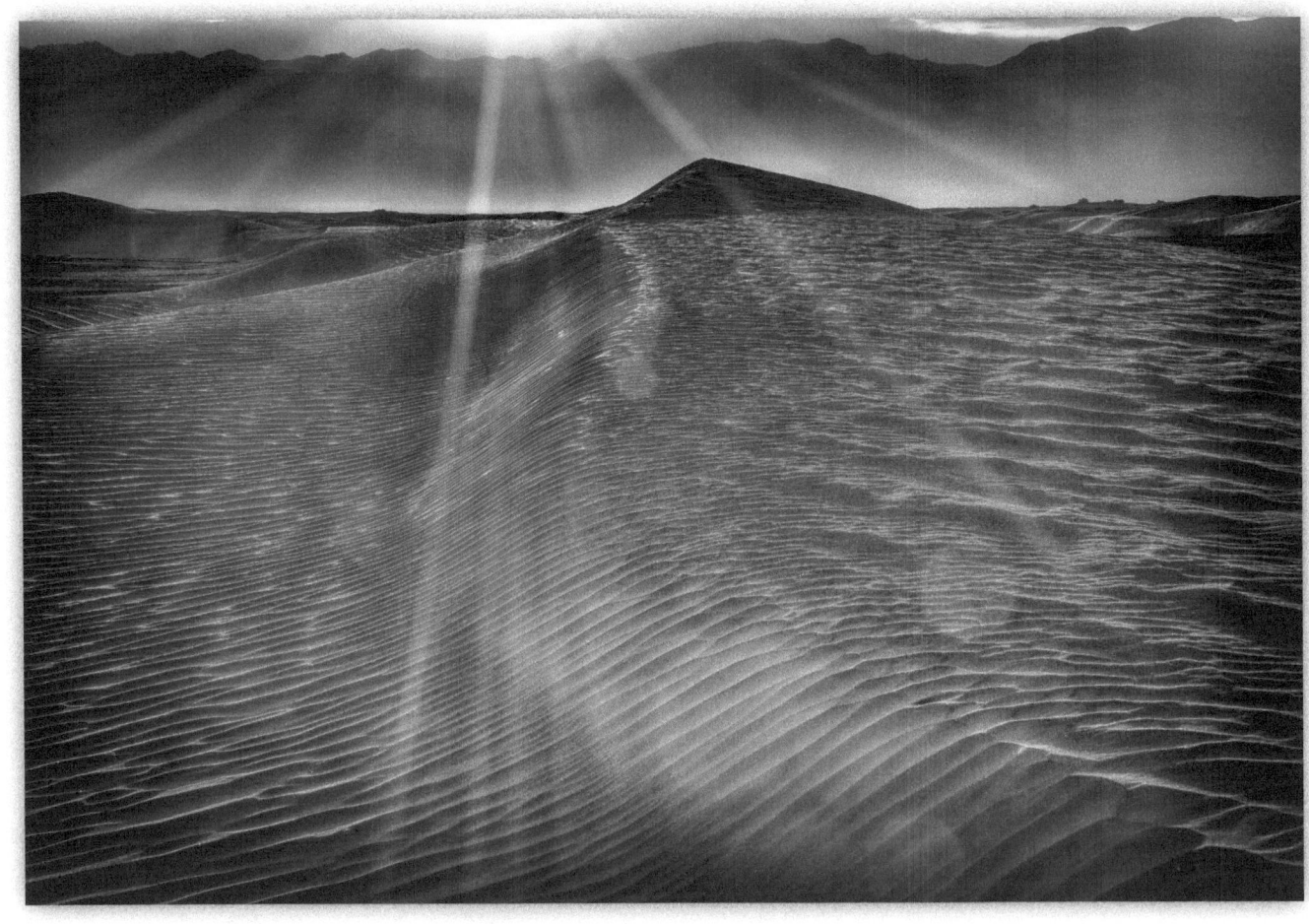

The wind had been blowing and there was lots of dust in the air. Visibility was poor at best even things close to me were in the haze of the dust. Looking to create a image was not real successful that late afternoon even the sun didn't develop much color as it headed down behind the Panamints. I setup anyway, putting the sun just out of the frame, and things started to get exciting. This image saved the evening and I went back to camp feeling that I had something for my effort.

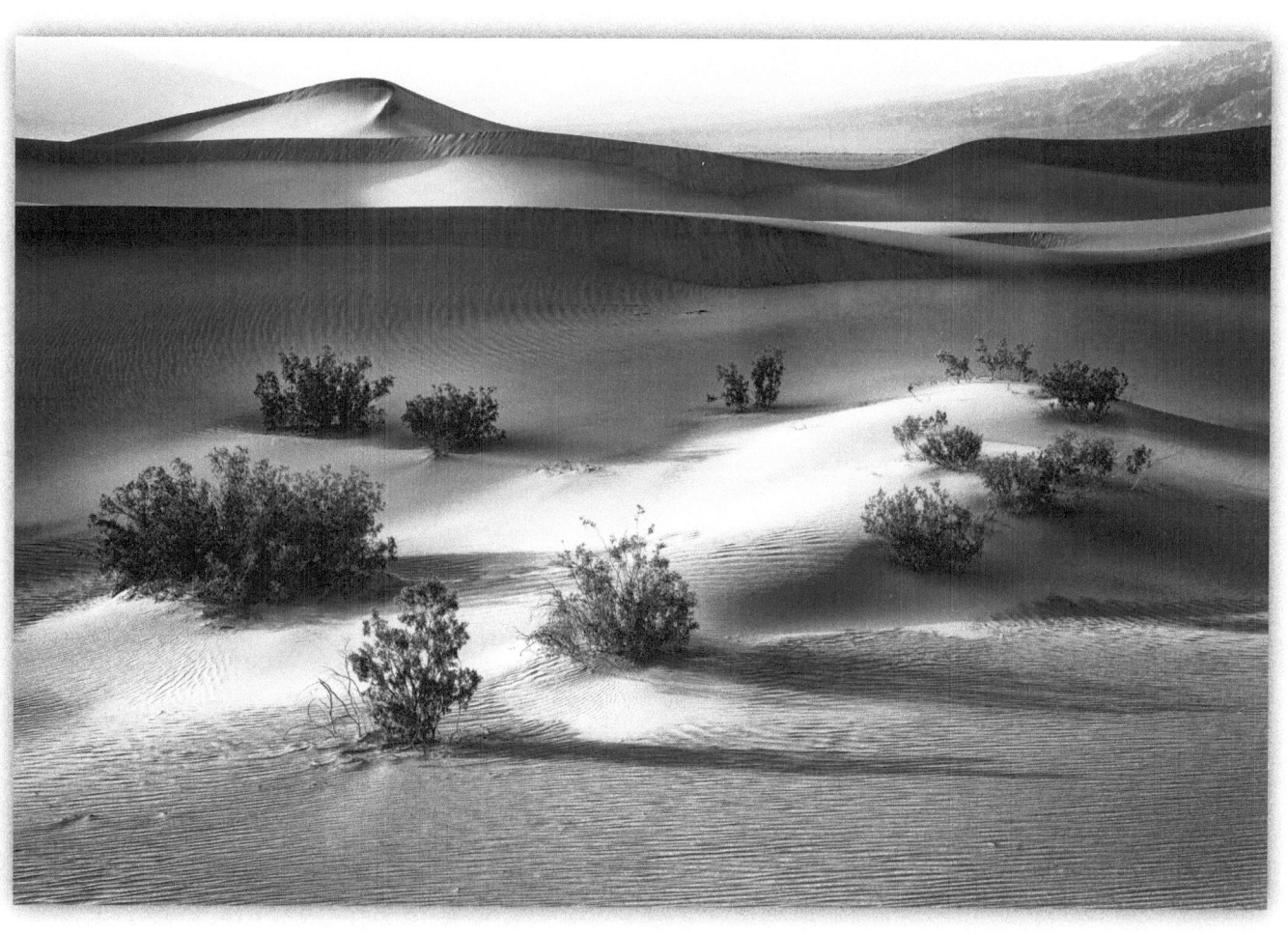

Beyond the dunes the dust was already blowing and in the dunes the quite light of sunset was just touching the surface. Wind will find the dunes this evening and erase the footprints left by man and in the morning they will be once again clean and fresh. That is the way of the mesquite dunes.

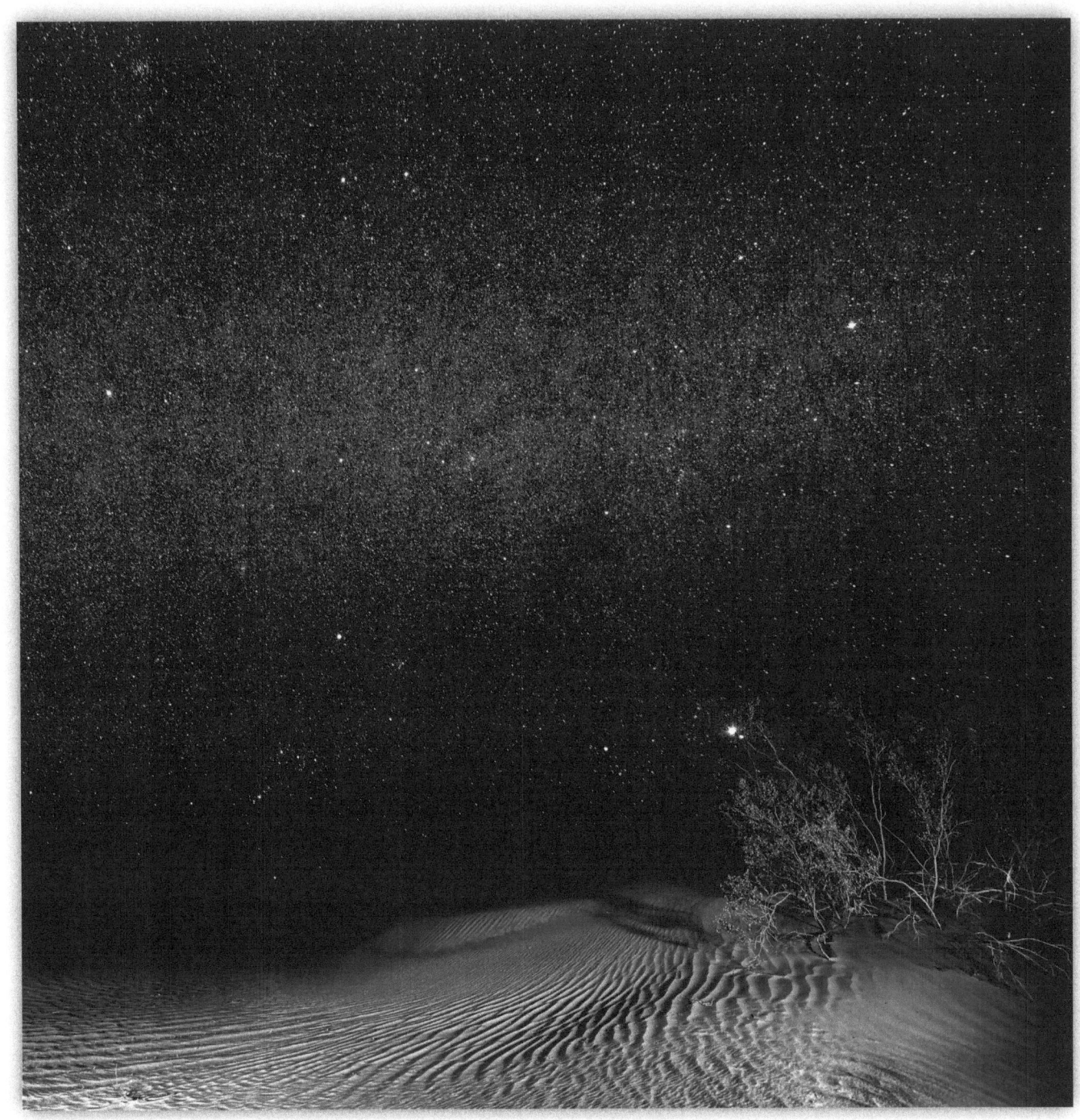

NIght

At night the dunes are a special place alive with activity. Animals both small and large come out in the cooler night temperatures. Walking in the dunes at night is a different experience moonlight gives a very soft feeling to the dunes and in the dark of the moon the stars are so close you fell like you can reach right up and touch them. When you walk with a flashlight at night the life in the dunes is revealed as you never thought it would be. On the night that I made this image a coyote tried to sneak by within a few feet. He ran when I said something as he knew I had spoiled his secret. I am sure he had happy hunting that night as I saw lots of kangaroo rats and field mice that evening. The Dunes are a magical place of which I will never tire.